Appalachian Homilies

Appalachian Homilies

Selected Essays from *Now and Then:*
The Appalachian Magazine

Roberta Teague Herrin

RESOURCE *Publications* · Eugene, Oregon

APPALACHIAN HOMILIES
Selected Essays from *Now and Then: The Appalachian Magazine*

Resource Publications
An Imprint of Wipf and Stock Publishers
199 W. 8th Ave., Suite 3
Eugene, OR 97401

www.wipfandstock.com

PAPERBACK ISBN: 978-1-6667-8475-6
HARDCOVER ISBN: 978-1-6667-8476-3
EBOOK ISBN: 978-1-6667-8477-0

VERSION NUMBER 06/04/24

Excerpts from "Archaeology" used by permission of the author, George Ella Lyon.

Essays collected in this volume used by permission of the Center of Excellence for Appalachian Studies and Services and East Tennessee State University.

"Mountain Spirits abide in Roberta Herrin's jewel of a collection of essays. From gathering wild cherries to sewing feed sack dresses to taking a deep walk in the woods, her essays resonate with the character, traditions, and often hard-won harmony of Appalachia. Many of the titles themselves tell a story. *Appalachian Homilies* offers a mix of insightful and thoughtful essays about mountain folk and their stories, including lessons we could learn a thing or two from in our time."

—**Michael Braswell**, author of *The Memory of Grace*

"These engaging and beautifully crafted essays offer both an insider's and outsider's perspective of Southern Appalachia. Roberta Herrin bears witness to her experience growing up in the mountains of east Tennessee in 'The Husk of Wildness,' 'The Mountain Farmer and Milton,' and 'Gold Is Not All.' Her voice is reverent, authentic, and clear. The other, equally compelling essays challenge blinkered notions of Appalachian 'otherness,' past and present. Natives and recent arrivals to the region will enjoy this book."

—**Anthony Cavender**, professor emeritus of anthropology, East Tennessee State University

"Though Roberta Herrin's essays in *Appalachian Homilies* encapsulate themes of previous editions of *Now and Then*, they provide a fresh opportunity to reflect on the past, ponder the present, and consider the future. Readers will be inspired to delve further into the marvels of Appalachia and perhaps be motivated to compose their own essays of new findings."

—**Sheila Quinn Oliver**, co-author of *Appalachian Children's Literature: An Annotated Bibliography*

"*Appalachian Homilies* should be required reading for all fans of *Hillbilly Elegy* and *Demon Copperhead*—as an antidote to the tired stereotypes those bestsellers rehash. Roberta Herrin's essays embody the qualities of many true born and bred Appalachian people: a quiet erudition, a deep spirituality, a penchant for humor and humility, and an abiding love for our beautiful, wounded mountains."

—**Lisa Alther**, author of *Kinflicks*

"Several years ago, Roberta Herrin was contacted by a Los Angeles reporter who was doing a story on cock fighting in Cocke County, Tennessee. His angle was 'Cocke County is the last little pocket of sin in the United States.' We all carry unconscious prejudices about Southern Appalachia, prejudices which Herrin dispels beautifully in an utterly non-pedantic way. I encourage you to read this book to understand Southern Appalachia in a way that is more honest than the stereotypes we picked up watching The Beverly Hillbillies."

—**Jeffrey Gold**, professor emeritus of philosophy, East Tennessee State University

Contents

Preface

IT WAS MY GOOD fortune to direct the Center for Appalachian Studies and Services at East Tennessee State University (ETSU) between 2004 and 2016. In that role, I wrote short essays for *Now & Then: The Appalachian Magazine*, which was a staple of the center for thirty-two years. Every issue centered on a theme—such varied topics as music, food, the environment, the Cherokees, and justice. Those brief essays make up this little volume of *Appalachian Homilies*. Initially my essays were labeled the "Director's Note," some of which are not included here because they focused on the workings and doings of the center, such as curriculum planning and development, staffing changes, and the center's component parts—the Archives of Appalachia and Reece Museum. Though these topics may have been of interest to the magazine's readers at that time, they are probably not of interest now.

Eventually, the "Director's Note" was changed to "Musings," a shift that gave me freedom to explore the theme of each issue more broadly and deeply. I could still include information about the center—as in "The Tending To," "We Cherish What we Cultivate . . .," and "Antidote to Agendas." I could also write about my own Appalachian upbringing and community—as in "The Mountain Farmer and Milton," "The Husk of Wildness," "When Cultures Meld," "The Spirit of Humanity in Appalachia"—and I was free to "muse" beyond the confines of Appalachia as a place on a map. "Be Still. Hear. Know." is a good example. Included in the music-themed issue, it could have accentuated the unique bachelor of arts in bluegrass, old time, and country music at ETSU, but information about that program had already been widely disseminated. I wanted to probe the theme from a more metaphysical perspective and encourage readers to think about music in nature—to think about the root of music. "Who Is Lady Justice?" appeared in the justice-themed issue, which contained essays about myriad *INjustices* in the Appalachian region; I wanted to explore the ancient symbol from another view and to ask, 'Who is she?" Is this ubiquitous symbol relevant in the twenty-first century, and are the ideals imbued in her applicable to a place where justice has been oft abused and ignored?

Ironically, as the essays took on a broader scope, they were also limited to 500 words. At first, this limitation felt like a curse, but as the process evolved, the constraint became a blessing. It forced me to be concise, to hone the prose, to compress ideas—as in the sonnet form. "The High, the Low, and the In-Between" is a good example. From the magazine issue devoted to "Appalachian high," the essay does not address the opioid crisis in the region or the view from high mountains; rather, it deals with our humanness: the space between the high and the low wherein we feel, appreciate beauty, and struggle with life's quandaries.

Essays are arranged in chronological order of publication. Some contain dated information, but updating would have warped the essays out of their original time—like "doctoring" a photo. As they stand, they provide a snapshot in time. For example, the reference to Twitter in "Is the World Really Flat, After All?" has not been changed to X. The *Encyclopedia of Appalachia* had sold 4,000 copies in 2006; today the number of copies sold and gifted is 11,618. Over twenty years, titles of academic programs and even the center's name have been revised. Staffing changed. People mentioned in the essays are no longer affiliated with the center. Sadly, some are now deceased, such as my mountain neighbors: Myrtle and Willard Elliott, Terry Hyder, and Dean Smith. Preserving the original "time" of the essays keeps my neighbors alive to me. It is a way to honor them.

Maintaining the original chronology provided an overview of my tenure in the center, and in the process, I noted a coincidence: This small volume begins and ends with essays about the past and the future. A character in the Maisie Dobbs mystery books, Dr. Maurice Blanche, says that "coincidence is a messenger sent by truth."[1] Is it mere coincidence that the past and the future are bookends for this collection, or does it signify that these concepts are rightly at the heart of Appalachian studies?

The final, longer essay "Appalachia 2061: Epiphanies and Revelations" was written after I retired and appeared in the last print issue of *Now & Then*. The magazine is now an online publication, which does not address specific themes but focuses broadly on the region. Its new title *Appalachian Places: Stories from the Highlands* represents this change in direction. According to the website, "The new format will allow us to reach a much wider audience and to include more content, including audiovisual resources. These changes will ensure that *Now and Then* [sic] will continue to be relevant for years to come."[2]

Appalachian Homilies is a paean to the old print edition of *Now & Then*. It is dedicated to all the people who supported the magazine for thirty-two years and fought to keep it alive through budget cuts, rising printing costs, and administrative changes—people who were devoted to its purpose and mission in the center and to its role in the Appalachian region. It is my sincere wish that this little volume will keep alive the original spirit of the publication that was once a cornerstone of the Center for Appalachian Studies and Services. May it stand alongside the new online version in service to Appalachia.

1. Winspear, *The American Agent*, 89.

2. *Now & Then: The Appalachian Magazine* https://www.etsu.edu/cas/cass/nowandthen/.

Acknowledgments

I GRATEFULLY ACKNOWLEDGE EAST Tennessee State University and the Center of Excellence for Appalachian Studies and Services for granting permission to reprint the essays included in this volume. I am especially indebted to Dr. Ron Roach, director of the center, for facilitating this permission.

I thank George Ella Lyon for permission to quote generously from her poem "Archaeology." She is always willing to share her work and nurture the work of others.

During my tenure as director of the center, Dr. Tony Cavender and Dr. Sheila Oliver kindly read the essays as they were written and published biannually. In 2024, these colleagues and friends were willing to give it one more crack. They have always improved the writing with spot-on observations and suggestions.

Finally, I am indebted to the hundreds of writers, editors, and staff members for whom *Now & Then: The Appalachian Magazine* was a labor of love spanning thirty-two years.

The Tending To

IN THE SUMMER OF 2006, we rolled up our sleeves and started packing our offices, getting ready to move from 209 Warf-Pickel Hall, which had been the "temporary" home to the center's administrative unit for seven years. The renovation of the former Sherrod Library building, vacant since 1999, was complete, and our moving date was set for July 17. We were eager to occupy new offices in one of the campus's oldest structures, space that was originally the reading room and stacks of the 1930s library. The architect wisely preserved parts of the original woodwork, including columns, pediments, transoms, dentil moulding, and doors. After two decades of depressing quarters and cast-off furniture, we were moving to a new home with all the professional appurtenances.

For several weeks, we sorted through twenty-two years' of files—the accumulated record of dreams, intentions, goals, hopes, failures, struggles, successes, and celebrations. Though faced with the need to sort, cull, and pack this material quickly, we could not work efficiently because each folder represented a chapter in the story of the center—handwritten, flip-chart notes from an *Encyclopedia of Appalachia* planning meeting; pink-pad telephone messages about a Ken Murray photograph for *Now & Then*; a grant proposal for a book on country music. We puzzled at the oddities, such as a classy business card from a former Ms Senior Tennessee; we marveled at the rarities, such as an archival photograph of Bob and Alf Taylor.

Suddenly it struck me that we were elbow-deep in the attestations of an institution—or were we? At what point does an entity such as a Center of Excellence become an institution? At what point can any organization or person lay claim to the label?

Some entities are institutions by their very nature, at least in Western cultures. Libraries, colleges and universities, hospitals, governments, churches, marriage—these have a kind of *a priori* claim to the label, a claim they have perhaps earned over centuries because they provide cultural support beams and trusses and cogs and engines and fuel. If institutions fail us, society collapses and personal chaos ensues.

People become institutions by the influence of their integrity, character, spirit, and wisdom, characteristics that ideally have their corollaries in public institutions. These human institutions are the cornerstones for hospitals and libraries and governments, and they are keystones that lock and bind the cultural arch of institutional purpose and human need.

After all, bricks and mortar do not an institution make. A hospital exists so that physicians and nurses can tend the body; a church so that clerics can tend the soul; a library so that readers can expand the mind. Among all these are people who tend the heart and the self. And therein may lie the defining feature of an institution: the tending to, as one tends a garden or a daughter or chickens or a pot on the stove. The act of tending requires patience, dedication, purpose, caring, love.

So when can the Center of Excellence in Appalachian Studies and Services call itself an institution? Is it enough that the administrative offices now occupy impressive and elegant space in Roy Nicks Hall (himself an institution)? No. Elegant space without purpose is hollow. Does the center's twenty-three-year presence merit the label? No. Longevity alone is not sufficient, though longevity is necessary. Perhaps productivity is the key. Can the center lay claim to the label because its archives is world-class; its Bluegrass, Old Time, and Country Music program is world-renowned; its museum is one of two accredited University museums in Tennessee; its Appalachian, Scottish, and Irish studies program is forging bright, new partnerships; its *Encyclopedia of Appalachia* has sold more than 4,000 copies?

Last July, as we sorted files and packed boxes, I felt like a Janus figure, casting one face to the past and one to the future, tending to both. Recently, as part of the center's ongoing strategic planning initiative, we established our commitments, and we chose the word *commitments* as opposed to *values* because commitments are forward-looking; they are concomitant with the "tending to." Here they are:

- To be a premier Appalachian Resource;
- To honor the diverse Appalachian culture and tradition but not be bound by it;
- To engage and challenge all constituents and each other on a deep level; and
- To raise questions and issues.

Whether the center is or ever will be an institution is rather a moot point, but if these commitments guide everything we do, then we will be tending our garden, tilling fertile soil for researchers, weeding through the region's past, acknowledging its flaws, encouraging its better qualities toward full bloom, and along the way, challenging ourselves to do our best work.

On a recent September morning, after the sorting and culling and packing and moving, all the center staff posed for a photograph on the steps of our new home in a venerable old building that has been preserved and refitted for a new generation's use. I was reminded of how important it is to save what is good, to keep it safe so that it can flourish from one season to another and its best elements can endure. And I was proud to be part of something called a Center of Excellence in Appalachian Studies and Services, made up of people who understand this importance, people who care about this region's history and commit themselves with caring and patience and love to tending its future. And that's what any institution worth its salt is all about—tending to the future.[1]

1. First published in *Now & Then*, Celebrating Appalachian Institutions, 22, no. 2 (2006) 2-3.

Digging Is an Act of Faith

THESE DAYS, EVERY ORGANIZATION, business, or institution crafts a mission statement, and far too many of us have spent weeks, months, or even years quibbling over words and paring down sentences, trying to fashion one tight word-package that communicates what we do. Don't get me wrong—mission statements are important. But I often think that our mission in Appalachian studies is so simple as to negate this tedious process. "To dig" might be sufficient: to delve so deeply into the region as to know its geology, prehistory, history, people, art, literature, music.

When I first heard George Ella Lyon read her poem "Archaeology," it struck me as a package of words that mirrors my search to "know" Appalachia—and my place in it. The poem opens with,

> I am digging
> With a soft brush   a pen
> at the site of my founding city
>   Mothers
>   Fathers[1]

A pen is as reliable a tool for digging as a spade or trowel. People who want to know a thing often write their way to the knowing. Words can burrow into the region, looking for certainties and secrets.

---

1. Lyon, "Archaeology," 27.

Like any good mission statement, Lyon's poem calls me back to it, again and again. I revisit it, the way one returns to an ancient spring to drink cool water from a cupped laurel leaf, or walks a worn path through familiar woods looking for newness—the first trillium of the season or the mole's soft, dirt-mound breaking up the old, hardened path. "Archaeology" has become a familiar and comfortable guide, pointing me in the direction of what matters:

> And the mountain speaks through its clay flute
> and feet dance up and down its back
> brushing off the light of this page
> to sift through dark rooms
> dust of a house I never entered
> by a window where I make my bread.[2]

Digging is an act of faith that we will find "something." Then we have to accept what we find under the surface and beyond the cliché, and what turns up may challenge our most fixed certainties. Brother Sim Mobberly comments in *River of Earth* that he used to think "a mountain was the standingist object in the sight o'God."[3] Like Sim, we have had to accept the impermanence of mountains, because mountaintops can be blown away. And remnants of long-extinct species can be unearthed, brought to life, as it were, in a new time, reminding us that all things exist in all time.

Can there be a nobler mission than to dig into the region in search of understanding, hoping to find the living interconnectedness of all things in all time: "dust of a house I never entered / by a window where I make my bread"?[4]

2. Lyon, "Archaeology," 27.

3. Still, *River of Earth*, vii.

4. First published in *Now & Then*, Digging Appalachia, 23, no. 1 (2007) 2-3.

The Husk of Wildness

ON A PERFECT SATURDAY morning in September, I am in Terry Hyder's potato patch by seven o'clock. It is a day to harvest. He is digging potatoes; I am gathering ground cherries. A wild delicacy, they grow late in the season on low vines, running close to the ground, hanging full of little paper-lantern sacs. Each sac starts out green and thick, but as the fruit inside matures, the lantern thins and fades to become a filigree, gray husk holding a golden "cherry." They like to grow among weeds in gardens that are on the down side of summer or along sunny roadsides or in fields after haying. A potato patch is the perfect spot.

In recent years, my neighbor Myrtle Elliott and I have pondered the scarcity of these treasures. She and my mother, Mabel, used to gather gallons of them for preserves, pies, and salads, but lately they're hard to find. So when I was meandering through the mountain fields and found ground cherries thriving in Terry Hyder's potato patch, I hurried down the road with the news, a mile or so, to Myrtle's house.

Straightaway, Myrtle told Terry that we wanted the ground cherries, and straightaway we hit a snag: Terry needed to mow off the patch so he could dig on September 22, and the cherries weren't ripe yet. (He didn't even ask why I was trespassing.) Myrtle and I said, "Well, maybe next year." A few weeks later, I was out "meandering" again and saw the newly mowed patch. I could hardly bear to look, but then I noticed that Terry had spared the ground cherries from his scythe, leaving little islands of green vines, a great inconvenience to him, a warm gesture to us neighbor women.

At seven o'clock on the 22nd of September, the air is chilly and the sun won't hit the field for another three hours. I stoop and pick, filling an old white enamel dishpan with golden fruit in brown-gray husks. I have hardly begun when Terry arrives on his tractor, and his brother Dean Smith and another neighbor, Jack Ingram, soon follow in their pickups. They get right to it. Terry plows out the straight rows of potatoes; Dean and Jack follow behind, raking them back into the furrow for easy pick-up. After just two rows, Terry stops the tractor and turns off the motor. We all look up to see him pointing to a fawn at the edge of the field. "It has come to check us out," he says. We are briefly still and watchful, and then we go back to work. Seeing that I can't keep ahead of the tractor, Jack helps me with the last few cherries growing in the patch, and I move to the vines on the edges of the field.

When the plowing is finished and the tractor is quiet, I can hear the conversation across the rows. The three men talk of the drought, bear season, the size of potatoes. Terry says that if you use liquid fertilizer the big potatoes won't get hollow. He picks up a huge potato, raps it with his knuckles, and there is no hollow echo; it is solid through. Myrtle thinks the potatoes will rot if he digs them when the moon is on the full; the time to dig potatoes is when the moon is waning and old. The "signs" are in the legs; we aren't sure what that portends for digging potatoes.

My harvest is done, but before I leave I offer them my labor, and it's a serious offer—I can sack potatoes—but they refuse me. As I'm loading the full pans into the car, Dean says, "Get you a good mess of potatoes out of this row." I do. Jack suggests that I might want to save some seed and plant my own little patch of ground cherries next year. "That's a good idea," I say, but we both know that I won't—and neither would he. It wouldn't be the same. The joy of finding them "in the wild" would be lost. These wild cherries are growing where they please, trespassing on a cultivated garden, and their wildness brought us to this moment, this gold, held in the filigree husk of Myrtle's wisdom, neighbors' generosity, the ritual digging of potatoes, the fawn, the conversation, the ephemeral bond among three people working on a little patch of earth at sunrise, and me on the edge of it all, holding tight.[1]

<hr/>

1. First published in *Now & Then*, Wildness, 23, no. 2 (2007) 2-3.

Affirming Urbanity
in Appalachia

THE THEME FOR THIS issue, urbane Appalachia, was suggested by Gwen Wallace, a native of Johnson City, Tennessee. Actually, she suggested "cosmopolitan" Appalachia, but we opted for the word "urbane." Some would argue that either word combined with "Appalachia" creates an oxymoron. We think otherwise. So in this issue, we listen to what people say about an overlooked characteristic of the region: urbanity. One person passionate about the topic is Mrs. Nane Dimmette Spainhour, who grew up in Lenoir, North Carolina, and lived in Boone for forty years. She now resides in Kingsport, Tennessee, where I visited her home to retrieve a collection of Lamar Stringfield materials she donated to the Reece Museum and the Archives of Appalachia at ETSU.

Stringfield was a flutist and Pulitzer Prize winner who grew up in Mars Hill, North Carolina. In his classical compositions and musical scores for outdoor dramas, such as playwright Paul Green's *Wilderness Road*, he borrowed motifs and themes from traditional mountain music. Mrs. Spainhour's sister, Laudie Dimmette Porter, studied flute with Stringfield in Charlotte, North Carolina, and regarded him highly as her teacher and mentor. The Dimmette family regularly enjoyed the company of musicians and artists in their home. (Percy Grainger dined in Nane's home when she was around twelve.) Nane's grandmother played the mountain dulcimer and taught her son to love music, so he saw to it that all his children had musical training. On Saturdays, he took a four-year-old Nane and her sister Dulcie to Salem College in Old Salem, North Carolina, for violin and harp lessons. Nane's interest in and exposure to artists and musicians grew after her marriage to David Spainhour, who had also studied the violin.

The violin did not "take" with Nane or David, but living among artists and musicians she observed the urbane qualities of mountain culture. Unfortunately, "People avoid writing about it when they write about the mountains." The region does not lack for examples of sophistication, urbanity, and all that these words imply, including education, but writers avoid the examples. A case in point is Cynthia Rylant's *Appalachia: The Voices of Sleeping Birds*, which implies that the region lacks educational institutions, even today. Rylant says that Appalachians have to "go off" to "find some way to become doctors or teachers."[1] Mrs. Spainhour, on the other hand, points to institutions such as Tusculum College, founded in 1794 in Greeneville, Tennessee, the twenty-eighth oldest college in the nation. The life of Kingsport attorney William Harrison Bowlin (1874 – 1956) is also proof that people do not have to leave Appalachia to become educated. Born on the North Fork of the Holston River in Fido, Virginia, he attended Beech Grove, a one-room mountain school; Kingsley Seminar in Bloomingdale, Tennessee; Shoemaker College in Gate City, Virginia; Emory and Henry College in Emory, Virginia; and in 1902 earned a law degree from U. S. Grant University in Chattanooga, Tennessee.[2]

Another writer who was blind to the urbanity of the region is Sir Arnold Toynbee.[3] Mrs. Spainhour wishes that somebody would "tell him to go. . . ." If he had ever visited among Appalachian families, he could not have advanced the notion that the upright Scots regressed when they settled in the region. Her life is testimony that regression is not a characteristic of the region. "Mountain people are not dumb," she says. "They have to be able to take care of any situation." While her family had little in common with the Snuffy

1. Rylant, *Appalachia*, 5.
2. Cooper, *Lawyer Will.*
3. Toynbee, *A Study of History.*

Smith icon, they were not privileged, either: "We had a garden, canned, cooked, washed our own clothes, and entertained. We were not waited on, hand and foot, though some in our community were. It's not good for people to be waited on, anyway." She believes that "intelligence comes from the use of your hands." That is why she insisted that all her children learn to weave.

Nane Spainhour would not apply the word "cosmopolitan" to Appalachians because it "denotes that anything is accepted." Mountain people are "hardheaded," have values, and do not easily conform. "Urbane" is a better descriptor. Though urbane people are not necessarily moneyed, they do have standards and "know the right things to do"—how to treat others and look people in the eye. Looking life straight in the eye, figuratively or metaphorically, may be a universal characteristic of urbanity, in art, in music, and in people, whether they live in the Midwest or Appalachia. Nane Spainhour can claim that characteristic, and so can Gwen Wallace—two native Appalachian women.[4]

---

4. First published in *Now & Then*, Urbane Appalachia, 24, no. 1 (2008) 2-3.

A Meditation on Fabric

During the 1989 Macy's Thanksgiving Day Parade, the American Cotton Growers launched an advertising campaign that has become a cultural classic: "Cotton, the fabric of our lives."[1] It is small wonder that this slogan has flourished for twenty years because it turns on a powerful metaphor—our lives as fabric, constructed of warp and weft. Pattern and weave. Selvage and fringe. Bias and grain.

Fabric is intimate. It swaddles, warms, comforts. Covers and protects. Compensates and disguises. Defines and announces. Fabric is at the heart of the stories of our lives—baby blankets, prom dresses, wedding dresses, shrouds. At the end, our lives stand on these stories—these memories:

> Swinging on the barn gate, waiting for the "feed man" to deliver chop for the cow and pigs, eager to see the sacks, hoping for a feed sack to match one already washed, ironed, and folded in the pantry. One feed sack can make a child's dress or an apron, with scraps left over for quilt pieces. Two or three or four of the same pattern can make curtains or a table cloth or a dress for a full-grown woman.

> Walking through Waechter's silk shop in Asheville, North Carolina, absorbing the smells of wool and dye and sizing, fondling the sturdy linens draped from the bolts, caressing the elegant silks, noting their "hand." A

1. Cotton Incorporated, Company Timeline.

Simplicity pattern or a Butterick pattern? Three yards or four? The high cost of a miscut. The embarrassment of a mismatched stripe.

The negligible importance of it all. The trifling seriousness with which we robe our bodies and adorn our homes as though the covering were all, forgetting what Henry David Thoreau taught us in *Walden*: "I say, beware of all enterprises that require new clothes, and not rather a new wearer of clothes."[2] Later in the same essay, he points out, "the very simplicity and nakedness of man's life in the primitive age imply this advantage at least, that they left him still but a sojourner in nature."[3]

Thoreau believed our lives should be birthed through our intercourse with nature, that nature be the fabric of culture. Is it possible that nature is the primary fabric of Appalachian culture? Ross Spears's four-part documentary *Appalachia: A History of Mountains and People*, which will be aired on PBS in 2009, interprets the region's culture through its prehistory and geology, relating the environmental history of the region and emphasizing the closeness to nature of its earliest inhabitants.[4]

The phrase "cultural fabric" includes much more than nature, however, especially when it describes regions. It suggests that spools of ethnicity, art, music, religion, and activism reel off diverse and colorful threads that together weave our culture, just as surely as diverse and colorful threads make the clothes on our backs, the cloths on our tables, the flags of our nations.

But "cultural fabric" also connotes more than the superficial warp and weft of nationality and class and privilege and conspicuous consumption. Appalachia's cultural fabric is built from the stories of Thoreau's "sojourners" who live by values that transform them into "new wearers of clothes." The transformation is usually the consequence of life-changing decisions, such as truth-telling, civil disobedience, or activism. I think of Denise Giardina's gift of words, of Bill Best's crusade to preserve

2. Thoreau, *Walden*, 20.

3. Thoreau, *Walden*, 30.

4. Spears, *Appalachia*.

heirloom seeds, of Helen Lewis's commitment to community, of Jeff Mann's willingness to tell his personal story, of Jack Spadaro's stand on mountaintop removal.

Feed sack or silk, the fabric is immaterial. The story is all. Rip out the weak stitch and sew a stronger seam. Cut across the grain. Embrace the ragged edge.[5]

5. First published in *Now & Then*, Fabric of Appalachia, 24, no. 2 (2008) 2-3.

Antidote to Agendas

THIS YEAR, THE CENTER for Appalachian Studies and Services celebrates its twenty-fifth anniversary. For the next few months, we will examine our achievements and successes, taking stock of what we do well and what we need to improve upon. One of the center's successes is *Now & Then* magazine, which has addressed a wide range of themes over the past quarter century—education, religion, music, stock car racing, the media, the Civil War, sports. It is fitting that this twenty-fifth anniversary issue of the magazine features food, which signifies prominently in every culture and no less in Appalachia.

Food is also a key ingredient in the culture of the center, whose faculty and staff work in four different buildings. We do not come together often, and when we do, it is usually for a business meeting of some sort. A monthly potluck lunch is the perfect antidote. Instead of working our way through an agenda, we fill our plates and enjoy the food.

Kirsti usually brings bread—whole-grain, healthy, hearty bread. At Thanksgiving, she fashioned the dough into a turkey-shaped, edible centerpiece. At Christmas, Constance brought a wonderful dish of baked butternut squash, dried cranberries, and nuts. April once brought curried pumpkin-peanut-butter soup. John usually brings pigs-in-blankets or soup beans and corn bread. Norma sometimes brings collard greens with potlikker. Randy brings pesto pasta or oriental slaw. Ruth makes smashed cauliflower with Boursin cheese. Jane makes a fabulous bread pudding, complete with potent hard sauce. We work happily through the afternoon after eating Jane's bread pudding.

Luck is usually with us at these events. Once, as the clock struck twelve noon, we were about to sit down to brown rice, apple muffins, and key lime pie, but within two minutes, Theresa and her museum staff appeared carrying bowls and pots that balanced out the meal. The truth is, we would have been quite satisfied with rice, muffins, and pie. Though food brings us together, it is not the main reason we sit at table.

Food is the catalyst for a type of discourse that cannot take place in formal, structured meetings. When staff, faculty, and students break bread together, we relax, tease, and laugh. We share stories and recipes. We come to know each other in ways not possible in organized settings.

The prime occasions of life are characterized by food—the wedding feast, with elegant tiered cake and fondant icing; the wake, with neighbors' roast chicken, scalloped potatoes, and red velvet cake; all-day singing and dinner on the ground, with the signature dishes of an entire community. Another such occasion is the retirement party. Our executive aide, Rachel, will retire soon. In place of the usual reception and speeches and plaques, she has requested a potluck lunch. We are delighted to oblige.

For the next quarter century, we in the center plan to keep our academic and administrative larders stocked with food. We will maintain our belief that agendas alone do not advance our mission and purpose; the laden table—communal, inclusive, democratic, bonding—serves us equally well. If food were a more frequent complement to the workplace, life would go better.[1]

---

1. First published in *Now & Then*, Appalachian Foodways, 25, no. 1 (2009) 2.

The Spirit of Humanity
in Appalachia

MY FAMILY HOMEPLACE SITS at the end of a dead-end road, in a bowl hollowed out of the mountains by some ancient force of nature. Visitors comment that they sense a presence on these acres. A few years ago, I invited colleagues for a workshop-retreat at the farm. An hour into the work session, Pauline quietly left the table to wander through the pasture and down the road. She said she had been "called away" from our mundane business to experience something larger, which she felt the minute she crossed the bridge and came into view of the house and field. One family friend senses spirits on the property—eyes that look out from the laurels along the creek bank. They watch and protect, she says.

Last year I met a man who has the "gift of sight." Like Sharyn McCrumb's character Nora Bonesteel, he "knows things." So I asked him, "What is it that people sense? What is this presence that called Pauline away from the work of the day? What are the spirits or watchers?" He said that people are picking up on the ancient energy of the mountains mixed with the accumulated spirit of all who have lived on the land. Energy and spirit emanate from eons of vegetative growth and rocks and water and pioneers and farmers and Native Americans—especially Native Americans, he said.

Perhaps this phenomenon—energy of the mountains mixed with centuries of human spirit—explains the universal attraction of all mountains, not just the Appalachian mountains. Greg

Mortenson captured it in *Three Cups of Tea*. Horace Kephart found it and documented it in *Our Southern Highlanders*.

It is tempting to think of mountain-energy-spirit as something extraordinary and otherworldly. The very word "spirit" connotes transcendence of the here-and-now. Phrases such as "pioneering spirit," "spirit of discovery," and "spirit of independence" describe the quality in human beings that lifts them beyond the ordinary. Even the word "moonshine" conveys a sense of lunar mystery. I would argue, however, that in Appalachia these are quite ordinary aspects of the culture, ordinary in the sense that they are hallmarks.

Over the past twenty-five years, *Now & Then* magazine has featured hundreds of essays and stories and poems about culture. But it is, ironically, the English poet and critic Matthew Arnold whose definition sits most comfortably with me. In the 1873 Preface to *Literature and Dogma*, he writes that culture is "the acquainting ourselves with the best that has been known and said in the world, and thus with the history of the human spirit."[1]

When visitors to my homeplace sense watchers or spirits or presences, they are witnessing culture, the accumulated spirit and energy of the past, the highest remnants of humanity. It is not otherworldly. It is immediate and sensible to us if we can be still and quiet in its presence. The Appalachian spirit is as old as the mountains and is reborn in every human being who is willing to become acquainted with it.[2]

---

1. Arnold, 1873 Preface, xix.
2. First published in *Now & Then*, Spirits of Appalachia, 25, no. 2 (2009) 2.

The High, the Low, and the In-Between

THE BINARY SYSTEM OF zeros and ones has created artificial intelligence and virtual worlds with avatars and farms, though virtual farms produce nothing akin to Jim Minick's blueberries or Bill Best's beans. The *Star Trek* android Data is the product of such a world. The perfection of artificial intelligence, he appears human in every respect but one: He cannot feel.

Human beings are also binary creatures living in a world of high and low, fast and slow, now and then. "Physical life is duple," writes Leonard Bernstein in *The Infinite Variety of Music*. "This is the symmetry our bodies are based on. We are creatures of the left and right, and in our center beats our heart, dutifully pumping its systole and diastole, 1-2, 1-2, as long as we live."[1]

Human beings naturally extend the meaning of these dualities, creating metaphors such as leftwing and rightwing that emphasize opposition and pull us toward extremes. On the one hand, the extremes are valuable. Rappelling from the 876-foot high New River Gorge Bridge would certainly shift my focus. When Jack climbed the beanstalk and entered the giant's world, he returned to the low ground with an "informed perspective."

On the other hand, there is danger in excluding the middle ground, the territory between the bridge and the river, the mountain peak and the valley. Jack's climb up that stalk and his rapid

1. Bernstein, *The Infinite Variety*, 92.

descent may have been more instructive than the view from the top. Synthesis takes place in the middle ground, which adds a third dimension to the dual world.

Bernstein does not overlook this third element. He explores the role of "tripleness" in music, arguing that the "three-concept is almost as fundamental as the two-concept." He emphasizes the word "almost" because "three . . . is *not* grounded in our biological nature. It is not *physical* in its function." Tripleness "is the first and noblest exception to our natural savage instinct of left-right. Three is an *invented* number; an intellectual number, it is primarily an *unphysical* concept. Perhaps that is why 3 has always been so mystical a symbol to man, as in the Holy Trinity."[2]

To an android, there is no in-between, wherein humanness is spawned. To be human is to understand simple opposites and, at the same time, traverse the complex middle ground that we call "grey area." How did we come to create so bland a term for the essential agent that transforms mere binary creatures into creative, struggling, feeling beings?

At our heart, we may be duple, but the triangle makes us human and mystical and spiritual. Appalachian high and Appalachian low and everything between comprise the Appalachian experience, which is not merely dual or oppositional but inclusive. Without the addition of an "emotion" chip, Data, the *Star Trek* android, can no more embrace the "high" of watching hawks from an old fire tower on the Blue Ridge Parkway than he can fathom the emotional contradictions of the Appalachian coal culture or suffer the "lows" of chemical addiction.

In the world of real farms, high mountains, blueberries, birds, and beans, we would do well to contemplate the irony of Bernstein's "intellectual," artificial, third number as the key to our *humanness*.[3]

2. Bernstein, *The Infinite Variety*, 95.
3. First published in *Now & Then*, Appalachian High, 26, no. 1 (2010) 2.

The Linguistics of Getting Around Appalachia

"GET AROUND." THE PHRASE denotes movement from one place to another, but it is also a common colloquialism. You might say, "I'll get around to fixing that hinge directly." (*Directly.* Now, that's a good word.) As a child, I was frequently admonished, "If you don't get around, we're going to be late!" In short, "You better hurry." Or you might ask, "How are you going to get around that problem?" The question could mean "How are you going to avoid that problem?" Or it could mean "How are you going to work that out?" There is also the conundrum: "I just can't get my head around that idea." Finally, the supportive connotation: "We need to get around that family and help them out."

In the seventeenth and eighteenth centuries, surveyor William Byrd got around. If you don't believe me, just read his *Secret Diary.* Though not an Appalachian, he penned a description in his now-famous *History of the Dividing Line* that stuck to the region: sloth, alcoholism, spousal abuse. Such characteristics of the "Lubberlanders" defined a region to avoid—to get around.[1] The same characteristics intrigued and, ultimately, invited the nation to "get its head around" Appalachia. Leisure travelers, botanists, and geographers traversed the region on foot, on horseback, by boat, and by wagon, hoping to fathom its unique features.

1. Byrd, *History of the Dividing Line,* 155-156.

Some famous Appalachians in the eighteenth and nineteenth centuries "got around," whether they knew it or not. The 1964 Beach Boys hit "I Get Around" could have been written for the likes of Daniel Boone and Davy Crockett who set out to find new territory when they felt the itch to wander and explore. They became well-known, well-traveled frontiersmen whose reputation for "getting around" Appalachia endures.

Concurrent with the Beach Boys number one hit (1963-1965), an entire federal agency, the Appalachian Regional Commission, was created that changed getting around the region forever. Without question, the ARC improved transportation. Without question, the ARC made it impossible to sidestep this chunk of United States geography. Since the mid-sixties, it has been impossible to disregard a region perceived to be isolated, poverty stricken, and vulnerable to myriad ills, from floods to mining disasters.

During the 1960s and 1970s, publications and organizations flourished in a movement to get around the region in every sense of the phrase: to traverse it, to define it, to explore it, to hurry it up, to understand it. Some of us get around the region to fend off inaccuracy, attack, or abuse, especially in the media. Remember the outrage in 1992 when the *Kentucky Cycle* won a Pulitzer and in 2003 when Dub Cornett proposed a *Beverly Hillbillies* reality show?

From the 1700s to the present, Appalachia has been a patch of ground to be reckoned with. Motivated by history, curiosity, passion, reverence, and, sometimes, plain old indignation, we get around Appalachia.[2]

2. First published in *Now & Then*, Getting Around Appalachia, 26, no. 2 (2010) 2.

Gold Is Not All

THE FIRST SIGN OF spring is not green but a hint of gold in the valleys. Willow trees along the creeks turn copper, then gold. The young, straight poplars stand like artists' brushes, their golden tips pointing skyward. Too soon, this early gold yields to green and retreats up the mountain sides, a wave of color and new life, washing up against rock and soil, finally crowning the trees with hearty, full leaves.

Robert Frost captures this phenomenon in eight couplets that begin, "Nature's first green is gold, / Her hardest hue to hold."[1] For Frost, the conversion of gold into green is a reversed sort of alchemy; every spring brings the sad news that brevity reigns, that all things, including perfection and life itself, are mutable: "So Eden sank to grief, / So dawn goes down to day. / Nothing gold can stay."[2]

Frost's poem appeared in the collection *New Hampshire*, which won the 1924 Pulitzer Prize for Poetry, so I hesitate to argue with such a venerated writer, but I have to say that gold is not all. Green is also good. The solid, dark green of zucchini and string beans is reliable. Gold can be fickle. After all, the promise of "gold" lured the extractive industries to Appalachia—timbering, mining, and now, drilling—and robbed the mountains and the people of their green. Perhaps the proper way to read Frost's

1. Frost, "Nothing Gold Can Stay," 905.
2. Frost, "Nothing Gold Can Stay," 906.

poem is to take the "gold" out of it entirely. Even in his couplets, gold resorts to trickery and diverts us from the real truth: "Nothing . . . can stay." Everything dies.

Unfortunately, emphasis on death can breed a strain of fatalism that erodes conscience and good sense, especially where ecology and the environment are concerned. What does one more plastic bottle in one more landfill matter? What does one more timber contract matter? What does one more blown-up mountain matter? If death is all, nothing matters.

The current emphasis on "greening" suggests otherwise: Everything matters. The only way to cheat death is to live thoughtfully in the moment and to cherish the first gold of willows and poplars as well as the full green of summer without anticipating the autumn reds and browns that will soon follow. Tender green shoots of polk root or the bitter leaves of branch lettuce are pure gold on the tongue *because* they are short-lived and can be had only in a brief season.

Spring greening invites us to live so respectfully in the now that all things are venerated and honored and protected. Greening requires us to witness every moment and every season in its fullness—the gold and the green and the autumn red and the winter grey. Pining for any one ephemeral stage, especially that early Eden, leads to eternal destruction. Let us cease to pine for gold alone and commit ourselves to the "greening" of the earth and of our consciences.[3]

3. First published in *Now & Then*, Greening of Appalachia, 27, no. 1 (2011) 2.

The Mountain Farmer and Milton

THERE WAS A FARMER in my community who was known to be a good manager of his fields and a good caretaker of his family. He was a godly man. He attended Sunday morning and evening church services and Wednesday prayer meeting. He was quiet and humble, plain of speech and dress; he had few needs and was not inclined to travel. When hunters or hikers came upon him in some solitary field or oak grove, on his knees, praying aloud, they left him undisturbed. He was not thought to be wealthy. It was said that he could not read or write.

When he died, his memorial service was held in a large funeral home chapel, not in the church where he took communion with his neighbors and washed their feet, where he shouted when he was filled the spirit. His wife and three daughters, knowing the truth of his eighty-nine years, understood that the small mountain church would not accommodate the great numbers who would come to honor him—not to mourn but to honor. While he lived, he received no public tributes—no service awards, no plaques, no gold watches—and had they been proffered, he would have been embarrassed.

The funeral service disclosed an extraordinary life that had appeared to be unremarkable. One after the other, people told stories of quiet generosity and deeds of service: He gave words of encouragement to the downtrodden. He slipped twenty-dollar bills into shirt pockets. He purchased a new suit for a young man who heard the call to preach but had no clothes fit for the pulpit. He gave the money to build a new church in a distant community. He mentored. He never bragged.

As I listened to each eulogy, I pondered the definition of "service" and the human craving for recognition. I thought of the great academic trio—teaching, research, and service—and wondered whether any act of service that is a contractual requirement can, in truth, be called *service*. I questioned what commonly passes for altruism. And, then, a line of poetry came into my head: "They also serve who only stand and wait."[1]

At first, these words from Milton's sonnet "On His Blindness" seemed inappropriate to the occasion of a mountain farmer's funeral. The persona in Milton's poem is a man whose blindness makes his "talent . . . useless," but this farmer had no infirmity that rendered him unable to serve. Quite the contrary: He served ably with all his "talents." And then I realized: To most members of his community, he *appeared* to stand and wait.

Milton's famous line of poetry settled among the eulogies delivered that day, becoming for me a tutorial on the nature of service. Because we do not know the quality or depth of another's service, we must take care not to judge it. In a world where public recognition is valued over humility, great acts of service go unnoticed every day: a suit of clothes, an uplifting word, a prayer in a solitary field.[2]

---

1. Milton, "Sonnet XIX," 168.
2. First published in *Now & Then*, Serving Appalachia, 27, no. 2 (2012) 2.

When Cultures Meld

IN 2001, ANTONIO WAS working as a dishwasher at El Matador in Johnson City, Tennessee, when he was introduced to Kathy. They talked. Kathy was moved by "Tony's" story—his hard life. He was from Guanajuato, Mexico, but found himself alone in East Tennessee, with no family. Kathy grew up in Carter County surrounded by a big, loving family.

Tony's father abandoned his mother and five children when he was ten, so he took a job milking cows to save the family from starvation and has never stopped working. Speaking little English, he came to North Carolina to mow yards. He has worked in the Christmas-tree industry and as a mechanic's assistant. He has cooked, installed insulation, and picked pecans, tomatoes, and oranges.

Kathy and Tony dated for a couple of years; then he went to Kentucky for a new job, and his life took a downward turn. He found himself living in a tunnel and sleeping on a cardboard pallet. One night he called Kathy and said, "If you'll come get me, I'll do anything for you." Kathy went, and after Tony returned to Tennessee, he made good on his promise. While she worked at Em's Restaurant, he cleaned her house and mowed her lawn. Their relationship deepened.

On Valentine's Day in 2007, Tony proposed marriage at El Matador, where they first met, and Kathy said, "Yes." They set a wedding date for December 29. On her wedding day, Kathy had to work. Her boss had told her she could leave early, but Em's was so busy she stayed until the two o'clock closing, and then she helped her mother Margaret set up the reception.

The wedding was the perfect cultural mix of people and food and music. Antonio grew up Catholic; Kathy was reared a Freewill Baptist. The marriage ceremony was performed by a retired Methodist minister in Little Doe Freewill Baptist Church. Kathy was pleased by how well the two families and the local community melded.

The seated, buffet reception was festive and fun. As guests entered the Little Doe Fellowship Hall, they first saw the tiered wedding cake, iced in white fondant. The buffet spread began with barbecued goat, tomatillo sauce, guacamole, rice, refried beans, and tortillas, prepared by El Torito Mexican Taqueria. Then came the ham biscuits; Little Smokies; chips and French onion dip; fruit trays of strawberries, kiwi, and pineapple; vegetable trays of cucumbers, broccoli, cauliflower, and ranch dip; a cheese tray with crackers; and a relish tray of olives and pickles— all prepared by Kathy and her mother. Coffee and orange-vanilla punch rounded out the menu.

Toward the end of the evening, the music and dancing began, but it didn't go long into the night. Mexicans dance at every opportunity, says Kathy; Freewills don't dance much. But this is an insignificant difference. What matters is that Kathy and Antonio have never encountered prejudice, and they continue to work hard so that every month they can send at least $100 to Mexico, which pays Tony's mother's electric and phone bills and buys groceries and medicine for her and the two children still at home.[1]

---

1. First published in *Now & Then*, Nuevo Appalachia, 28, no. 1 (2012) 2.

Is the World Really Flat, After All?

WITH THE ADVENT OF television in the 1950s, linguists feared that regional dialects would disappear and everyone in America would sound like Walter Cronkite, Edward R. Murrow, and Eric Sevareid. Similar concerns grew with the advent of the Internet and social media in the late twentieth century. Would distinctive regional cultures disappear? Regions are defined by geographic boundaries (maps) and cultural markers, such as food, music, narrative traditions, art, dance, and language. Will the Internet, YouTube, Facebook, Twitter, and cell phones erode or strengthen regional identities?

Such questions prompted Thomas Friedman to write *The Lexus and the Olive Tree* in 1999, followed by *The World Is Flat* in 2005. Friedman acknowledges that "the flat-world platform . . . has the potential to homogenize cultures." On the other hand, he believes that this "flat-world platform" has "an even greater potential to nourish diversity to a degree that the world has never seen before. . . . The flat-world platform enables you to take your own local culture and upload it to the world." We live in an age that "globalizes the local."[1]

In a 2006 essay, Bill Ivey and Steven Tepper take Friedman's thesis one step further: "Today's consumer," they argue, "is not bound by old [19th-century] hierarchies." Ivey and Tepper believe that "today people define their status by consuming as omnivores

1. Friedman, *The World Is Flat*, 477-479.

29

rather than as snobs." Technology and the Internet have toppled the "old hierarchies," freeing individuals to search the globe at will and consume whatever whets their interests and appetites, be it education or music or art or real-time cultural experiences in another hemisphere. Ivey and Tepper call this phenomenon the "curatorial me," the modern individual who can exercise personal tastes and interests to "curate" diverse experiences from unlimited and global choices (B6).[2]

Friedman, Ivey, and Tepper could easily have predicted Massive Online Open Course (MOOC), which provides free online education. MOOC students do not enroll in a university, do not pay fees, can "curate" a set of courses to meet their intellectual interests and needs, and do not earn a degree or a diploma. Harvard, Stanford, MIT, Princeton, and the University of Virginia are among the elite participants in this initiative, which has stirred controversy and outright fear in the academy.

How will these twenty-first-century global applications of technology affect Appalachia? Will issues that have plagued Appalachia for decades, such as access to affordable education, be eradicated? MOOC is now available wherever the Internet reaches; at the same time, students who desire a traditional campus experience can easily "curate" or choose from options on the opposite side of the globe. A perfect example is the Iranian student who found Bluegrass, Old Time, and Country Music Studies via the Internet and plans to enroll at ETSU in spring 2013.

Will a "flat-world platform" enrich or diminish regional identity? Will regionalism disappear altogether in the grab-bag, "curatorial me" approach to understanding a diverse world? As a region, are we prepared to wrestle with the questions?[3]

2. Ivey and Tepper, "Cultural Renaissance," B6.
3. First published in *Now & Then*, Global Appalachia, 28, no. 2 (2013) 2.

Idleness and Industry

AT AN EARLY AGE, I learned that industry (with a lower-case "i") was the cornerstone of human worth, the foundation of our daily lives, our reason to exist. Nobody in my community ever took a vacation. Cows had to be milked. Pigs and chickens fed. Beans picked. Had we known Isaac Watts's poem "Against Idleness and Mischief" (1715), we would have agreed with it. Better known as "How Doth the Little Busy Bee," the poem enjoins us to keep busy, like the bee, lest our idleness be used for evil ends: "For Satan finds some Mischief still / For idle Hands to do."[1]

By the nineteenth century, Industry (with a capital "I") had changed the nature of work and the concept of idleness. Watts's premise became the subject of ridicule, as in Lewis Carroll's *Alice's Adventures in Wonderland* (1865). When Alice tries to recite Watts's preachy little poem, it comes out all wrong: "How doth the little crocodile / Improve his shining tail."[2] In Wonderland, Watts's ideas about idleness are rendered nonsense. Industry and mechanized processes theoretically freed workers from manual labor and provided "free time," so the word *idleness* morphed into *leisure*. How could leisure be the devil's tool, when it had been won by hard, Industrial work?

None of this discourse mattered in my home. We continued to believe that idleness and outright sin were good buddies, if not

1. Watts, "Against Idleness and Mischief," 65-66.
2. Carroll, *Alice's Adventures in Wonderland*, 15.

close relatives, so it was vital to demonstrate (Dare I say *flaunt*?) industry. To prove our worth, we gave visitors a tour of the cellar with its shelves of canned beans and tomatoes, crocks of pickled corn and kraut, and bins of potatoes and apples. We showed off Mama's quilts. She trotted out the Dutch Doll, Lone Star, Drunkard's Path, and the crazy quilt, with all our names embroidered on its irregular swatches. Privately and to each other, we marveled at our own work. I recall standing at the window with Mama, watching Daddy mow a field of hay. "Look at how your daddy mows," she said. "See how the hay falls in neat rows. Nobody can swing a scythe like Lee."

In addition to farm work, my father also worked in Industry at North American Rayon Corporation (NARC) in Elizabethton, Tennessee. Locals called it "The Plant." In the history of the Appalachian region, "industry" is romanticized, and "Industry" demonized. Without question, workplaces such as NARC could rival idleness as a tool of the devil that devalued human worth. But my father and thousands of Appalachians like him didn't debate the virtue of industry over Industry. They took equal pride in mowing hay and making rayon, and they had neither idle time nor leisure time. Whether NARC valued my father's work was beside the point. *He* valued it.

At a recent lecture by George Collins on the history of the Magnavox Company, the audience included former Magnavox workers who did not demonize the company but were emotional and passionate about the televisions, radios, record players, and fine cabinetry they made. Their work in Industry gave them worth. At bottom, the man or woman who recognizes the connection between work and self-worth won't debate the distinctions among idleness, leisure, industry, and Industry. They are just glad to be busy, to be doing useful work, keeping clear of the devil's playground.[3]

---

3. First published in *Now & Then*, Appalachian Industry, 29, no. 1 (2013) 2.

Be Still. Hear. Know.

AT THE APPOINTED HOUR, leave your cell phone inside the house and lock the door as you depart. Halfway down the path, do not look back. Remember Lot's wife? Do not return to unlock the door and pocket the phone. Take a risk and unfetter yourself from the Disney-bright icons, the metallic ring tone, the human voice, and the purr of the digital machine. Disengage for a spell. You will not dissolve into the great void but will stay solid and sentient. Solipsism has no place where you are going. This is a day for music, not metaphysics.

Walk deep into the woods and seek out a flat rock at the foot of an old tree—oak, walnut, or giant hemlock will do. Sit. Settle your back against the rough bark, and welcome the slight discomfort that will tether you to wakefulness. Breathe deeply. Smell the leaf mold that feeds the forest. Feel the energy of photosynthesis, oozing tree resin, pumping mouse heart, churning earth worm.

At first, your brain clutter will override the red squirrel's chatter in the canopy. He is tuning up and worried. The swell of his fretting will soon redirect your self-focus, and you will wonder what woodland crisis he protests. When the strident crow joins his alarum, you know they have hit upon a singular motif—ridding the woods of *you*. But don't leave. If you stay very long and very still, their notice will abate, and they will settle into their own harmonies while *you* disappear—to them and to yourself. In this transcendent state you will hear the mountain symphony, Opus I, *The Genesis of Knowing*: The tremolo of twin birch trunks, bark scraping bark. The thud of black walnuts striking the undergrowth. The staccato of a hen turkey's cluck. The riffs of the bird chorus.

When fog moves in, the audible mist strikes leaf and stone in a mass of nothingness. The wood wind is counterpoint to the crackle of leaves stuffed into the gray squirrel's mouth. Hear the scratch of her claws on trunk and limb as she rises to her tree-nest, builds it against the coming cold, and descends. She will repeat this movement to perfection—do not applaud at its end.

Now you are more alive and real than you have ever been while manacled to twitters and buzzes and mechanical voices that are transmitted but not transcendent. Now you are witness to the music of the spheres—not Pythagoras' mathematical harmonies but the wild hymnody that anchors the self to the source of all knowing, the source of all music.

At the coda, rise and stretch. Offer a grateful bow to the players, and next week or tomorrow, at the appointed hour, leave your cell phone inside the house and lock the door as you depart. Halfway down the path, do not look back. Remember Lot's wife?

Be still. Hear. Know.[1]

1. First published in *Now & Then*, Music in Appalachia, 29, no. 2 (2014) 2.

Civil Words and Civil Wars

On September 21 through 23, 2006, Emory & Henry College celebrated the twenty-fifth anniversary of the Appalachian Literary Festival with an assembly of seventeen noted Appalachian writers. Amid this festival of words—well-chosen, finely-honed, and civil words, even in disagreements—I discovered Ann Olson's handmade greeting cards. One in particular caught my eye. It bears Olson's photograph of Civil War diaries from 1863, 1864, and 1865, below which she has penciled the caption "Civil Words."

Having long admired this Appalachian photographer's work and thinking of the many uses for "civil words," I bought a goodly supply. In the eight years since, these cards have borne missives of apology for hastily-spoken words. They have urged relatives to forgive well-meaning words that, nevertheless, led to feuding among kith and kin.

I may have expected too much of an humble greeting card— and my own missives, for that matter. At the drop of a word, families bound by love and blood and tradition can erupt in outright warfare. Against their own best interests, businesses, governments, and even churches succumb to irreparable schisms ignited by uncivil words—or words *perceived* to be uncivil.

In any exchange of words, perception is key because words are capricious little things. They can leave the lips clothed in simple attire but arrive at the listener's ear wearing an offensive get-up that signals war. Or perhaps it is the capricious ear that willy-nilly transforms blameless words into artillery. Regardless, the ensuing melee is decidedly uncivil. (Frankly, "civil war" is a misnomer and an oxymoron.)

If words can spark civil wars, can civil words prevent civil wars? Are peace-making words less compelling than war-mongering words? I think not. I believe in the power of diplomacy and arbitration and "civil" discourse, all of which are presently in short supply, from the Appalachian coal fields to the US Congress.

The need for civility is so great that the National Endowment for the Humanities (NEH) made it a priority. Beginning in 2009, on the eve of the American Civil War Sesquicentennial, NEH Chair Jim Leach launched his American Civility Tour with a simple message: "Civilization requires civility. . . . Words matter."[1] Words, he said, "clarify—or cloud—thought and energize action, sometimes bringing out the better angels of our nature, sometimes baser instincts. . . . Conversely, healing language such as Lincoln's plea in his Second Inaugural address for 'malice toward none and charity for all' . . . can uplift and help bring society and the world closer together."[2]

Another American who understood that words matter was Benjamin Franklin. In his 1787 "Speech in the Convention," he argued for ratification of the Constitution and enjoined every man in the Convention to "doubt a little of his own infallibility."[3] At age 81, he was prudent enough to know that the proper clothing for words is humility.

I suggest that words in themselves can neither incite nor avert war; rather, the self-awareness of the speaker and listener—their willingness to admit fallibility—directs words toward their mark. In the discourse of conflict, the most effective words are clothed in humility, a cloak that safeguards meaning when words travel between the lips and the ear. Humble words have power—the power to foil uncivil wars.[4]

1. NEH, "NEH Chairman Jim Leach," Press Release.

2. Leach, "Words Do Matter," 30.

3. Franklin, "Speech in the Convention," 271-272.

4. First published in *Now & Then*, Civil Wars in Appalachia, 30, no. 1 (2014) 2-3.

Who Is Lady Justice?

YOU SEE HER EVERYWHERE—VIRGINAL Lady Justice, also known as Scales of Justice and Blind Justice. An amalgam of Roman, Greek, and Egyptian mythologies, she is a lofty symbol with mutable interpretations. She typically carries a set of balance scales in one hand and a two-edged sword in the other. The blindfold, which appeared in the fifteenth century, led to the phrase "Justice is blind."

This symbol is ubiquitous and nuanced, both lofty and familiar. Lady Justice adorns hundreds of public structures, from Appalachia to the Middle East, wherein the law is applied and justice is meted out: the Marion County, West Virginia, Courthouse; the United States Supreme Court Building in Washington, DC; the Tehran Courthouse in Iran. She is also a popular-culture figure, available in statuary for purchase on e-Bay and Amazon. A rock band has appropriated her name, as did Neil Gaiman for his 1995 *Lady Justice* comic book. She is everywhere on Facebook, where readers borrow her image and her name and post apt commentaries and quotations.

Having made her way into pop-culture, this universal symbol is a natural target for parody and satire. She has been portrayed in countless cartoons, one of the most notable being the November 2, 2006, cover of *Rolling Stone*—"Inside the Worst Congress Ever"— which depicts an assemblage of corrupted characters emerging from a cracked-open US Capitol dome. Among them is a voluptuous Lady Justice, balance scales held high in her right hand, but her left hand has dropped the sword to lift the blindfold for a wide-eyed peek at the chaos around her, suggesting, perhaps, that even the virginal, innocent Lady Justice is subject to corruption.[1]

Rolling Stone and other satirists, cynics, and cartoonists who distort this icon do us good service. They force us to examine what these symbols mean—female (virgin), balance scales, blindfold, sword. Like most universal symbols, these are commonly taken for granted.

Would a male figure, for example, prompt different subtexts? Just how significant is the gender of an icon? How significant is her virginity? The scales, on first thought, make perfect sense. In the pursuit of justice, evidence is "weighed in the balance." But what is the function of blindness where the evidence is concerned? Would justice be better served if Lady Justice could see—with eyes wide open—what tips the balance? Evidence, too, can be corrupted—manufactured. A blind Lady Justice cannot *see* the *what*—she can only feel the weight. Does "just" evidence weigh more or less than "corrupt" evidence? And does she ever use that sword? Does she protect the innocent or punish the guilty? How does she know the difference if she is blind? Or does the sword imply—sadly—that decisions about law and justice are naturally partnered with conflict, if not outright battle?

What is legal may not be just, and what passes for justice in one century may be unjust—and illegal—in another. Still, Lady Justice endures as an ideal—a belief that "justice for all" can be realized. Can it? Of course not. Lady Justice may be innocent, impartial, objective, and blind to prejudice, but *we* are human. It is *our* blindfold that slips; *we* wield the sword to ill purpose; *we* tip the balance scales with greed and self-interest.

It is good that Lady Justice is blindfolded. Otherwise, she may throw down the scales and sword and flee the hundreds of buildings she adorns, leaving us with bare, unembellished structures—and bereft of hope.[2]

1. Grossman, Cover Illustration, *Rolling Stone*.
2. First published in *Now & Then*, Justice in Appalachia, 31, no. 2 (2015) 2.

We Cherish What
We Cultivate

DURING THE 2004-2005 ACADEMIC year, the Center for Appalachian Studies and Services celebrated its twentieth anniversary
with a series of public programs, including a symposium on the
Media and Appalachia. Rick Bragg was the keynote speaker, and
there were sessions on the environment, healthcare, TVA, the
War on Poverty, and the Appalachian Regional Commission, but
the session that drew the most attention was called "Hollywood
and Hokum."

Dee Davis, then president of the Center for Rural Strategies,
debated Dub Cornett, filmmaker and documentarian, who had
proposed a reality TV show modeled on *The Beverly Hillbillies*.
Dub had sold the idea to CBS President Les Moonves and had even
found an Appalachian family willing move to Hollywood to star in
the series, but public outrage—including invective from the floor
of the US Senate—derailed the idea. At the symposium, Cornett
made a strong case, arguing that he "never intended for the series
to lampoon his own people. . . . Jed Clampett had integrity. The
banker was an idiot." But Davis won the faceoff when he pointed
out that, Cornett's intentions aside, Jethro Bodine was a twenty-
six-year-old sixth-grader and in one episode he thought he had
turned Granny into a chimpanzee. The Davis-Cornett debate got
front-page coverage in the *Johnson City Press* (April 15, 2005) and
stirred controversy. One man was outraged that the center invited

Cornett to campus, much less to participate in a symposium. To my mind, it was exactly what a center of excellence ought to do: cultivate dialogue about Appalachia.

Even more successful than the symposium was a series of film screenings from collections in the Archives of Appalachia. For example, "Historical Images from Elizabethton" was held in the town's old Bonnie Kate Theater. (In 2015, the theater was listed as one of the Tennessee Preservation Trust's Ten in Tennessee Endangered Properties.) The evening included footage of the 1929 North American Rayon Corporation strike and featured the Melton Barker film *The Kidnapper's Foil*, which Bradley Reeves had found in the Bonnie Kate some months earlier. On the night of the event, a line of people stretched through the lobby, outside the building, and down Sycamore Street. Refusing to turn anyone away, we held three consecutive showings. What we learned that evening informed our work for the next decade: Communities cherish historical and cultural programming that accurately reflects their identity.

Perhaps the most enduring marker of this twentieth-anniversary celebration was a broadside featuring Don Johnson's poem "The Latin Root for *Cultivate* Means *Cherish*." (Anita DeAngelis designed the broadside and printed it in her garage on her Vandercook press.) I will not parse Johnson's poem, though I do like to contemplate the juxtaposition of the green, sprouting "winter crop" and "hard loaves" stacked in windrows.[1]

At the time the broadside was printed, center staff and faculty were engaged in hard work—the lengthy, tedious process of strategic planning. We labored over the usual mission, vision, commitments, and purposes. Someone suggested that an apt vision statement might be, "It's not your grandfather's Appalachia anymore," and I still think that would have sufficed, but we failed to grasp the two words that were right there in front of us—*cultivate* and *cherish*. Though we did not consciously adopt those two words as our mantra, they became imbedded in a work plan that guided

---

1. Johnson, "The Latin Root," 35–37.

the Center for the next decade—two words as inextricably linked to our mission as they are linked by etymology.

To carry out our plan—to meet our commitments and purposes—we cultivated all the assets of the Center: Regional Resources Institute, Reece Museum, Archives of Appalachia, *Now & Then* magazine, and—most importantly—the faculty and staff. Together we worked at the small tasks and the big tasks, but the one achievement I am most proud of is the curriculum: a minor and a bachelor of arts in bluegrass, old time, and country music; a graduate certificate and a master of arts in Appalachian studies; and an academic Department of Appalachian Studies to house them.

A decade has passed since that 2004-2005 celebration, and the center celebrated its thirtieth anniversary in 2015 by hosting the annual Appalachian Studies Association Conference. The 900 attendees enjoyed more than 600 presentations in 150 sessions. Though the words *cultivate* and *cherish* appeared nowhere in any printed conference material, I believe that they were the implicit motivation for those 900 attendees.

Motivation comes in all sorts of guises. Consider, for example, a phone call I received from a *Los Angeles Times* reporter who wanted my help with a story on cock fighting in Cocke County, Tennessee. "The angle that I am taking for my story," he said, "is that Cocke County is the last little pocket of sin in the United States." *Really?* I thought. *The last little pocket of sin. Right here in Appalachia.*

As I look toward retirement on June 30 and look back at a dozen years of the center's hard work, that phone call sticks in my memory. It affirms our mission and my 2004 decision to bring Dub Cornett to campus. It makes me glad for the controversy sparked by his debate with Dee Davis. After all, Hollywood is still promoting Appalachian hokum. Universities still need to cultivate and cherish their communities. When the need arises to write a vision statement, we should listen to our poets.[2]

2. First published in *Now & Then*, Cultivating Appalachia, 32, no. 1 (2015) 3-4.

Appalachia 2061: Epiphanies and Revelations

THE EIGHTEENTH-CENTURY WRITER EDMUND Burke is often quoted as saying, "Those who don't know history are destined [doomed] to repeat it," but there is no solid evidence that he ever said it at all. Versions of this statement are attributed to several writers, most notably Winston Churchill: "Those who do not learn from history are doomed to repeat it." Alas, there is no evidence that the statement can be credited to Churchill, either. George Santayana's iteration, however, can be documented: "Those who cannot remember the past are condemned to repeat it."[1] The popularity of the quotation and frequency of its misattribution are significant: Human beings are invested in the past, and the statement implies that ignorance of the past makes for a dark future.

Writers such as Eckhart Tolle, on the other hand, caution us to live in "The Now." In *A New Earth* and *The Power of Now* he argues that focus on the past or future is ego-driven and unwise. On a personal, spiritual level, Tolle's advice may be sound, but I wonder whether it serves agencies, policy makers, and organizations such as the Appalachian Studies Association (ASA) who want to make a viable future for the region.

On the ASA website, I found good fodder for discourse about Appalachia's future, especially in the annual conference archives. Except for 1981, every ASA conference has had a theme,

1. Santayana, *The Life of Reason*, 284.

and collectively they tell us what is important to the organization's leadership and membership—community, change, diversity, mountains, culture, place, rural and urban Appalachia, and, not surprising, the future.

In 1978, the first ASA Conference theme had asked the logical question, "Where Do We Go from Here?" In 2008, the Association continued to look forward: "The Road Ahead: The Next Thirty Years of Appalachian Studies." ASA had just completed a two-year strategic planning process, so the theme was—again—logical. Both of these themes may apply to the Association more than to the region; regardless, they suggest that this organization is intentional about Appalachia's future.

In conference themes between 1978 and 2008, the future continued to signify. In 2001, the theme was "Standing on the Mountain, Looking to the Future." Considering that phrase and the year 2001, I immediately thought of Stanley Kubrick and Arthur C. Clark's classic movie (and subsequent novel) *2001: A Space Odyssey*. Their masterpiece was released in 1968, the same year that Martin Luther King delivered his prophetic "mountaintop" speech.

And then I had an epiphany: In the 1960s, as mountaintop removal was gaining the momentum and support to destroy the core metaphor of King's speech—the mountaintop—Kubrick and Clark were creating new metaphors for the future—dreams. Their imagined future was a piece of science fiction grounded in the past—in prehistory. These interwoven strands of history and current events and fiction and popular culture had not been apparent to me in 2001 or in 1968, for that matter. They became obvious only after the passage of several decades—only by looking backward from the future.

Next I considered the 1982 and 1986 themes. "Futures: Past and Present" initially struck me as a conundrum. Could there be past and present futures? Could there be plural futures? And then I had a revelation: George Orwell predicted that, indeed, there *could* be. Ironically, these two years straddled the title date of Orwell's futuristic novel *1984*, which is a reversal of the year in which Orwell completed the book—1948. (It was published in

1949.) The 1986 theme—"Contemporary Appalachia: In Search of a Usable Past"—also seemed like a conundrum: What does it mean to have a usable past?

A USABLE PAST

Orwell's dystopian future requires a malleable, alterable past that is certainly not what ASA conference leaders meant by a "usable past." Orwell's main character, Winston, works in the Ministry of Truth rewriting old news stories to reflect the government's constantly shifting versions of reality. His must "rectify" the past, making it consistent with the present: "This process of continuous alteration was applied not only to newspapers, but to books, periodicals, pamphlets, posters, leaflets, films, sound tracks, cartoons, photographs—to every kind of literature or documentation which might conceivably hold any political or ideological significance."[2]

Winston excels at this task, even enjoys it occasionally, but a simple, critical question nags at him: "How could you communicate with the future?"[3] His answer is to begin a diary, not knowing for whom he is writing it, knowing only that he must. It is, of course, his undoing. In Orwell's future and in every authoritarian society, writing that records independent thought and action, even privately, is dangerous. Why else would the destruction of books be central to so many dystopian novels (*Fahrenheit 451*, 1954) and depictions of Nazi Germany (*The Book Thief*, 2005)? The unalterable printed word is a menace to dictators and tyrants and ideological bullies.

The key word is "unalterable." Preserving "every kind of literature or documentation" in its original content and form also preserves the full range of human thought and action, including compassion, altruism, fallibility, and evil. Santayana is correct: Recorded history represents a usable past because it connects us

---

2. Orwell, *1984*, 39-40.
3. Orwell, *1984*, 6.

to the lowest and highest examples of our very humanness and, consequently, helps us understand how to "be."

As Winston struggles to be human—through self-expression, love, a simple paperweight, a private tryst in the woods—he comes to understand that a usable past exists also in the minds and memories of the people, in their humanity: "What mattered were individual relationships, and a completely helpless gesture, an embrace, a tear, a word spoken to a dying man, could have value in itself. The proles, it suddenly occurred to him, . . . had stayed human."[4] Orwell's proletariat—the "proles"—are, ironically, the only citizens who remember the past: the only people alive, thinks Winston, "who could give you a truthful account of conditions in the early part of the century."[5] The proles vaguely remember the old culture, such as songs and children's lore, and though they still have a weak tether to community (they gather at pubs to drink beer, for example), their tether to humanness is vanishing.

Winston believes that the "real" past also exists in "solid objects,"[6] such as his diary and his treasured, antique—and prohibited—paperweight. Artifacts of material culture are infused with memory and evoke feeling: clothing, tools, household goods, art—everything from shoes and butter churns to dolls and typewriters. In other words, the stuff of archives and museums.

In the 1960s and 1970s, the "old Appalachian culture" was celebrated through folk festivals and heritage days that featured "old timey ways," but these gatherings have fallen somewhat out of fashion. If demonstrations of quilting, splitting wood, making apple butter, drying apples, baking bread, churning milk, forging horse shoes, crafting furniture, etc. are passé in 2016, how much less important will they be in 2061?

I am not arguing for a revival of these celebrations, but they did serve a good purpose: They connected the present and past through material culture and memory, reminding us of the value of practical knowledge, common sense, and self-reliance—the value

4. Orwell, *1984*, 165.

5. Orwell, *1984*, 87.

6. Orwell, *1984*, 155.

of being able to "figure things out" and "do stuff." In *1984*, common sense is the "heresy of heresies."[7] These gatherings may also have exposed a human frailty: "Old timey ways" were synonymous with hard work, and we like a future where machines and government do all the heavy lifting. Orwell's proles fell into this trap.

I believe that people still exist—especially in Appalachia—who can "do stuff": dowse for water, build a barn, make a dress, devise a manual pump, grow potatoes, dry apples, kill and dress a chicken, fry it up, and figure out a use for its feathers. They can "rig up" all sorts of gismos to get the work done without once whipping out a cell phone to Google instructions. Before computers complicated the four-stroke internal combustion engine, every community had such as person in the revered "shade tree mechanic." People like this are a threat to Big Brother and the Party.

HAL AND BIG BROTHER

Did works such as *2001* and *1984* foretell the extinction of the shade tree mechanic? Has this community hero been replaced by Kubrick and Clark's computer, Hal 9000? Maybe. Hal is being fully realized in IBM's artificially intelligent Watson, who appeared on *Jeopardy* in 2011 and, more recently, assisted with diagnoses and treatment protocols at the University of North Carolina Cancer Center.

Has Orwell's omniscient, omnipotent Big Brother been realized through technology? I recently sat through a discussion about the benefits of Facebook for businesses: branding a company, tracking customers, and marketing to them based on their Internet activity—all without their knowing it. The person sitting beside me whispered, "Orwell's Big Brother is watching us."

Indeed, he is. Sometimes we applaud him, as when "security" cameras help protect personal property, recover children in Amber Alerts, and identify terrorists. More often we quietly acquiesce to his sinister intrusions: monitoring our Internet

7. Orwell, *1984*, 80.

activity, e-mails, and cellphone calls or photographing our earthly property via satellites and drones.

Such acquiescence again brings to mind Orwell's proles. Winston thinks, "If there was hope, it *must* lie in the proles."[8] But he is disappointed. Proles will never—can never—revolt because they are passive and because "The rule of the Party is forever."[9]

MAKING A VIABLE APPALACHIAN FUTURE

Using Orwell's trick of reversing 1948 to create 1984, I am trying to envision Appalachia in 2061, trying to fathom a strategy to thwart "Party rule" and create a sustainable, humane future. "'Who controls the past,' ran the Party slogan, 'Controls the future: who controls the present controls the past'"[10]

Lest this essay begin to sound like a doomsday alarm or a rallying call to Luddites, let's be clear: The Hals and Watsons *will* shape Appalachia's future, and frankly we are already dependent on them, but they do not have to *be* the future. We do not have to abdicate to them our usable past, our humanity. But how do we coexist with technology and stay human?

1. Read widely in all genres; entertain divergent viewpoints, including ancient and current, regional and universal, liberal and conservative. This reading should embrace conflicting versions of history, from revisionist works to historical fiction.

2. View multiple Appalachian images, historic and current—photographs, motion pictures, documentaries, posters, art, cartoons.

3. Know the organizations that study, document, and interpret the region. Not all of them will resonate with you, and that's

8. Orwell, *1984*, 69.
9. Orwell, *1984*, 261-262.
10. Orwell, *1984*, 34.

as it should be. Only in a dystopian society would all people be expected to embrace all Party-approved organizations.

4. Be savvy about technology. Know how to use it, know how not to be its pawn, and know how to "be" without it.

5. Learn how to "do." Plant a seed, build a fire, cook a meal, climb a mountain, make something—anything—using your brain and hands and feet.

6. Learn how to be comfortable and happy alone, and protect the spaces that are outside the watch of Big Brother. In these private, quiet places, listen to birds and water and wind—listen to your own heartbeat.

7. Keep a diary, write letters, and hold on to the letters you receive. In your Last Will and Testament, bequeath these to an archive.

8. Nurture and sustain Appalachian archives and museums.

9. Revere, honor, and learn from the remaining shade tree mechanics in your community.

10. Venerate "individual relationships, . . . a completely helpless gesture, an embrace, a tear, a word spoken to a dying man"[11] over any security and ease that the Party and technology can provide.

To create a sustainable future for Appalachia, we must live thoughtfully and spiritually in the present moment, as Eckhart Tolle advises. However, living in "the now" does not preclude a firm grasp on a usable past. Perhaps a slight rephrasing of the oft-quoted cautionary statement is apt: "Those who are out of touch with a usable past will not enjoy a benevolent future." Edmund Burke wrote, "You can never plan the future by the past,"[12] but without that usable past, we have no roadmap.[13]

11. Orwell, *1984*, 165.

12. Burke, *A Letter from Mr. Burke*, 73.

13. First published in Now & Then, The Future of Appalachia, 32, no. 2 (2016) 13-15.

Bibliography

Arnold, Matthew. *Literature and Dogma*. 1873 Preface. Hessen, Germany: Outlook Verlag 2023.

Bernstein, Leonard. *The Infinite Variety of Music*. New York: Simon & Schuster, 1966.

Burke, Edmund. *A Letter from Mr. Burke to a Member of the National Assembly* 2nd ed. London: J. Dodsley, Pall-Mall, 1791. https://ia800906.us.archive.org/18/items/aletterfrommrbuooburkgoog/aletterfrommrbuooburkgoog.pdf.

Byrd, William. *History of the Dividing Line*. In *The American Tradition in Literature*, edited by Sculley Bradley et al., Vol. 1, 155-156. New York: Grosset & Dunlap, 1974.

Carroll, Lewis. "How Doth the Little Crocodile." In *Alice's Adventures in Wonderland / Through the Looking-Glass*, 15. Garden City, NY: Nelson Doubleday, n.d.

Cooper, Ann Goode. *Lawyer Will*. Boone, NC: Parkway, 2004.

Cotton Incorporated, Company Timeline. https://www.cottoninc.com/about-cotton/history/company-timeline/#1980.

Grossman, Robert, artist. Cover Illustration, *Rolling Stone*. November 2, 2006.

Franklin, Benjamin. "Speech in the Convention." In *The American Tradition in Literature*, edited by Sculley Bradley et al., Vol. 1, 271-272. New York: Grosset & Dunlap, 1974.

Friedman, Thomas. *The World Is Flat*. New York: Farrar, Straus, Giroux, 2005.

Frost, Robert. "Nothing Gold Can Stay." In *The American Tradition in Literature*, edited by Sculley Bradley et al., Vol. 2, 905-906. New York: Grosset & Dunlap, 1974.

Ivey, Bill, and Steven Tepper. "Cultural Renaissance or Cultural Divide?" *The Chronicle of Higher Education* 52 (2006) B6.

Johnson, Don. "The Latin Root for *Cultivate* Means *Cherish*," *Bridgewater Review* 25 (2006) 35-37. https://vc.bridgew.edu/br_rev/vol25/iss1/15.

Leach, Jim. "Words Do Matter: A Conversation with the Chairman." *Kentucky Humanities*. Spring 2011, 29-32.

Lyon, George Ella. "Archaeology," *Catalpa* 27. Lexington, KY: Wind, 1994.

Milton, John. "Sonnet XIX: When I Consider . . ." ("On His Blindness"). In *John Milton: Complete Poems and Major Prose*, edited by Merritt Y. Hughes 168. New York: Odyssey, 1957.

National Endowment for the Humanities, "NEH Chairman Jim Leach Continues the American Civility Tour." Press Release. January 11, 2010.

Orwell, George. *1984*. Orlando: Harcourt, 1977.

Rylant, Cynthia. *Appalachia: The Voices of Sleeping Birds*. New York: Harcourt Brace, 1991.

Santayana, George. *The Life of Reason: Reason in Common Sense*. New York: Scribner's, 1905.

Spears, Ross, and Jamie Ross. *Appalachia: A History of Mountains and People*, DVD. University Park, MD: James Agee Film Project, 2009.

Still, James. *River of Earth*. Lexington, KY: University of Kentucky Press, 1978.

Thoreau, Henry David. *Walden*. New York: Signet, 1960.

Tolle, Eckhart. *A New Earth*. New York: Penguin, 2016.

———. *The Power of Now*. Novato, CA: New World Library, 2004.

Toynbee, Arnold. *A Study of History: Abridgement of Volumes I-VI*. Abridged by D. C. Somervell. New York: Oxford University Press, 1974.

Watson, Sam. "Hillbilly Hokum." *Johnson City* (TN) *Press*. April 15, 2005: 1, 10A.

Watts, Isaac. "Against Idleness and Mischief." In *The Oxford Book of Children's Verse*, edited by Iona and Peter Opie, 49-50. Oxford, UK: Oxford University Press, 1994.

Winspear, Jacqueline. *The American Agent*. New York: Harper, 2019.

General Index